Dogs
Unleashed

ORVIS®

Dogs Unleashed

ADVENTURES WITH OUR BEST FRIENDS

FOREWORD BY DAVE PERKINS
AND NANCY MACKINNON

Guilford, CT

An imprint of
Rowman & Littlefield

Distributed by NATIONAL BOOK NETWORK

British Library Cataloguing in Publication Information Available
Library of Congress Cataloging-in-Publication Data Available
ISBN 978-1-4930-2679-1 (hardcover)
ISBN 978-1-4930-2680-7 (e-book)

Designed by Alison Wilkes

♾™ The paper used in this publication meets the minimum requirements
of American National Standard for Information Sciences—Permanence of
Paper or Printed Library Materials, ANSI/NISO Z39.48-1992.

Contents

PHOTO: MITCH KOWALSKI

Foreword

by Orvis Vice Chairman Dave Perkins
and his wife Nancy Mackinnon

IT IS JUNE IN VERMONT. Our truck is in the driveway with the back down and the roof box open. It is packing time before we head west for the summer, and our four dogs know exactly what is happening. Their message to us is clear: they are not going to stay behind. They track us from room to room, and are close on our heels as we trundle outside with our belongings. For added insurance, they may decide to curl up on one of the dog nests laid out in the truck, and they might not move for six hours. Truth is, we wouldn't dream of leaving without them (we hardly go to the grocery store alone). Despite the hassles of moving such a crew cross-country, our home is hollow without them.

We spend much of our lives outdoors, and there is hardly an experience that isn't better if the dogs are with us. A hike in the woods is almost certainly a moment to enjoy, but with our dogs it is an adventure, an exciting exploration of new and old.

LEFT It's no secret that all the members of the Perkins family are serious dog lovers.

Four generations of English setters and two black Lab sisters live with various members of the Perkins family.

Their boundless curiosity and joy draws us a little more deeply into the moment. No matter how many times we hike the same area, they exude even more enthusiasm on the next outing. Oh, to be so optimistic.

And what would a bird hunt be without our dogs? Certainly less productive, but also less fulfilling. There is nothing more glorious than watching our pointing dogs course across a landscape with determination, and then suddenly lock up without a doubt about what they smell. Our Lab will then wait patiently behind us as we walk up to the point, and if we are lucky enough to have a bird fall, we turn and release her. We can't hide our pride as we watch her tear past us, seeing nothing except the spot where the bird went down. We realize that is the ideal, but it happens often. Even when they make a mistake and bust a covey, point a meadowlark, or retrieve a decoy from a duck pond, we all, dogs included, share a good laugh and move on.

When you enter our home, there is no doubt that it is a dog home. There is the unabashedly warm greeting and competition for a pat as you edge across the

threshold. Then there are numerous dog beds of all sizes and descriptions. Most friends wonder if the beds are primarily for visitors because, yes, our dogs are often found on the furniture. Claim a seat early, or you might have a tough negotiation with a doleful pup. Hard to say, "Move." Their toy basket starts out piled high with squeaky toys, rubber toys, marrow bones, and antler sheds, but watch your step because it doesn't stay that way. We should have hazard signs in our house. At dinner, begging is not tolerated, and the dogs honor that. This doesn't mean they don't squeeze between chairs and through legs to find a napping spot under the table for the duration. They make great toe-warmers, whether it is a chilly fall evening or a hot summer night.

Our life with dogs isn't about perfection. It is about experiencing wonderful places with our closest companions, and maybe learning to be in the moment and treasure it almost as much as they do. It is about cuddling on the couch, embracing their love, and hoping against all odds that someday we will live up to their expectations.

Dogs Unleashed

EVEN THE MOST ADVENTUROUS OF US ARE UNLIKELY TO EXPLORE THE
world as thoroughly as a dog. That spirit, that sense of wonder, understanding, and adventure, has been the tether that binds humans to their most trusted animal companions, because there is no journey that can be taken alone that is as satisfying as the same path in the company of a dog. Whether it is a hike, or an errand, or even just a nap on the couch, things go better, and our appreciation of things goes deeper, when we get to experience it all with a dog.

Is it simply their superior intuition? They seem so often to be pointing us away from where we think we should be headed. Well-trained dogs are supposed to stay by our sides, but perhaps better trained dogs know when to interject their own

LEFT Dogs always seem to be pointing us towards the unbeaten path.

ideas into a task. No, they seem to be saying as they head just slightly off the path at first. This way, they want us to know, will be better. And it usually is.

Nothing gets past them. The dog's sense of smell is between 10,000 and 100,000 times stronger than our own, which is why they take such keen interest in that one dull leaf or that damp mound of dirt at which they insist on pausing, pressing their noses close as if they were sommeliers assessing a fine Bordeaux. The world itself turns their senses on. The wind can literally tell them things. No wonder then, that after taking in so much, they spend the majority of the day napping, filing all that micro-data away in their brains.

ABOVE A dog's nose is many times more sensitive than our own.

A sense of wonder of the outdoors has tied humans and dogs together for thousands of years.

"I think we are drawn to dogs because they are the uninhibited creatures we might be if we weren't certain we knew better."

—GEORGE BIRD EVANS

There is no journey that can be taken alone that is as satisfying as the same path in the company of a dog.

In her poem, "Her Grave," the writer Mary Oliver mourns the loss of one of her own dogs and celebrates her athletic hunting prowess, "her great and lordly satisfaction at having chased something." We watch our dogs bounding from the indoors, into the yard, across fields, slopping with relish in the mud and through chilly streams of water, rolling on a fresh patch of grass or a dank pile of autumn leaves. We watch them with a degree of the same euphoria they express every day in their dog lives, while at the same time we know, as Mary Oliver does, that compared to them and their dog sensibilities, "we know almost nothing."

True dog lovers share this sense of awe and respect for the canines that share their life. To be in synch and share such a wordless, daily sense of communion

> "Dogs do speak, but only to those who know how to listen."
>
> —ORHAN PAMUK

comes surprisingly close to the divine. There is understanding that is genuinely mutual, and this reciprocal aspect of our relationships with dogs is probably the most difficult to fathom for those who haven't experienced it firsthand. This deep connection is what makes our dogs feel like such an essential part of our families. We don't share blood or language, but our bond goes beyond that in ways that reinforce a sense of belonging together, of understanding, and of appreciating the mystery we each must feel about the wonder of our coexistence.

As dog "owners," we spend much of our time learning how we might teach our dogs, and how we might work with them to fit them into our ideas of what the world looks and feels like. But imagine the possibilities if we were to think at least as often

Our deep connection with dogs is what makes them such essential family members.

A kayak ride is so
much better in the
company of a dog.

of the ways we can learn from them. We can attribute much to the dog's advanced sensory perception, but it is also clear that one of the nearly magical skills of these animals is that they actually pay attention to the sensory information they receive. They don't ignore the world's signs or signals (unless, perhaps, it is when their master is telling them it is time to come in). They don't wear headphones. They don't assume that anything can be left to doubt (except, perhaps, their spot on the couch). They know to be cautious around strangers; they know never to doubt friends. They know, without pretense, that this is living.

This may be the secret that solves the mystery of why dogs and people were made for each other: dogs can, if we let them, connect us back to the natural world around us. They can point us to our own intuitive nature to observe and explore

BELOW By land or by water, dogs never stop exploring.

and wonder. Dogs can remind us that life, lived properly, is often very messy. And they know that for every sprint, we deserve the time to curl up and nap as well. As Edward Hoagland once wrote, "In order to really enjoy a dog, one doesn't merely try to train him to be semi-human. The point of it is to open oneself to the possibility of becoming partly a dog."

A toast to dogs! To their boundless curiosity. To their dedication to athletics—and their elevation of napping to the level of sport. To their making the most of every season, from icy winters to muddy springs, sweltering summers and perfect falls. To their mischief-making and their admirably short supply of shame. To their remarkable

"Dogs are better than human beings because they know but do not tell." —EMILY DICKINSON

> "If I could
> be half the
> person my
> dog is, I'd
> be twice
> the human
> I am."
>
> —CHARLES YU

A dog's enthusiasm for
exploring the world
comes without shame.

work ethic (when they are working) and their ability to cast work aside when they are done. To their companionship and ability to listen when all of our other best friends fail. To everything they teach us in exchange for the little bit we teach them.

But most of all, here's to their uncensored, fearless dedication to exploring, whether the territory is the countryside around us or what we thought was a child-proof cabinet in our house. For dogs, there is nothing that isn't worthy of investigation—and celebration. They can even find wonder in our discarded socks. They

"What a dog feels, a dog shows, and, conversely, what a dog shows, a dog actually does feel." —JEFFREY MOUSSAIEFF MASSON

view the world as a place of equal opportunity . . . for digging, tasting, rolling, chewing, marking, tugging, snoozing, playing, fetching, and smelling. And beyond all of that, for loving every moment that they share with us.

No wonder we love them so hard back.

They spend every moment reminding us of the wonder of being alive and our good fortune to be in this world together.

The Back-to-School Dog

"YOU LEFT, NOT I," SUSAN MINOT WRITES AT THE START OF HER POEM "Family Dog." Imagining life from the dog's perspective, she shows us how his life is a series of losses as the family children grow up and move on. It's a melancholy poem, but also an apt reminder of how our relations with animals, even in childhood, are framed by arrivals and departures.

Autumn seems to be a particularly doggish time—the days grow shorter, the nights colder, and all across the land children leave their summer of playtime and go back to school. No more mornings spent welcoming a succession of siblings as they come out to breakfast on their own schedule; no more tricking each of them into thinking you haven't been fed yet. No running through sprinklers or chasing a game

LEFT The fall is a bitter-sweet time for dogs.

of kickball. Fewer visits from neighbors and cousins and all kinds of children still wet and smelling of the neighborhood pool.

What is a dog to do? As for the rest of us, this particular change of seasons warrants a change in priorities. Fall is time to refocus, take up new hobbies, chew new bones. And wait through the afternoons for everyone to come home.

Mornings may be briefer, but their frantic pace is exhausting. For a family dog, the responsibilities are rigorous and awesome. Watch the frenzy of morning showers and bewildering attempts at grooming; lie beneath the breakfast table and make careful note of anything that goes unconsumed. Watch for the bus. Watch the

ABOVE Dogs wait patiently for their kids to come home and play.

"The best way to get a puppy is to beg for a baby brother—and they'll settle for a puppy every time."

—WINSTON PENDLETON

Parents love their kids, but rarely do they provide the joy of reunion that dogs provide.

children waiting for the bus. Bark as the children disappear. Then keep your eyes fixed on that spot long after they have gone.

Like good dogs, children enjoy a regular routine, and for families with dogs, one of the joys of being dismissed at the end of a day of classes may be the greeting one receives upon returning home. Let's face it, parents love their children, but rarely do they express the joy of reunion that dogs provide every weekday afternoon. There they are, at the bus stop, or watching with anticipation from the window, never turning away because to do so might break the spell that is luring their children back home.

ABOVE LEFT Reading to dogs is great practice for reading to others in school.

ABOVE Getting creative with leaves: a timeless afternoon tradition.

The stereotype is true: dogs sometimes do eat your homework. But they also keep you company while you do it, resting at your side or at your feet while you finish reading that particularly difficult passage that has been assigned. Dogs make such great teaching assistants that they have even been used to help teach reading aloud. They may not understand the words, but dogs love to hear the sound of our voices, and they never make the mistake of interrupting or correcting a child. They make reading fun, and studies have shown that programs that allow young readers to practice with dogs boost the students' confidence.

School also brings meaning to holidays, when everyone is home—and food is plentiful. What would a holiday table be without a hovering dog? Even Halloween seems important in the canine worldview: all of those curiously dressed creatures

Dogs and school days make holidays even more exuberant.

Dogs are always teaching us through their curiosity and caution.

"From the dog's
point of view,
his master is
an elongated
and abnormally
cunning dog."

—MABEL LOUISE ROBINSON

Dogs, like children, enjoy
routine, which for them
usually includes a walk.

walking the streets and ringing the doorbells, appearing and disappearing again. Tradition and repetition teach us these things: how to be part of a community, how to have fun, how to interact with and appreciate the differences around us. And dogs are always teaching us the same things; we know what they love without question, and their curiosity and caution about the world form our own ideas as well.

It's a shame we can't always have a dog at our side as we advance our education. Helen Keller, who was deaf and blind after a childhood illness, was given a companion dog by her classmates at Radcliffe. Phiz, as he was called, was so bonded with her that he often escaped to find her as she climbed aboard a streetcar or even attempted to join her in the classroom for a Shakespeare lecture. These days,

ABOVE It's a shame that we can't always have a dog at our side.

ABOVE Our dogs can be an anchor for our childhoods.

while dogs may not be welcome in dorm rooms, the calming presence of animals has been used to help students hold it together during finals, with service dogs and shelter pets coming in to visit and offer that comfort that only good dogs can.

We start our relationships with dogs as their teachers. Whatever our age may be, they look to us for cues, and they think everything about us, even our flaws, is genius. No wonder we love them back. But one of the most poignant moments in our lifelong relationships with them is that moment when they mature beyond our own years. In dog years, they become senior to us. In the blink of an eye, they are ten or twenty years older than we are. And apparently wiser, too.

What great teachers dogs are, in our childhood, and beyond.

"The dog is a yes-animal, very popular with people who can't afford to keep a yes-man."

—ROBERTSON DAVIES

In the blink of
an eye, our dogs
are suddenly
older than we
are.

In the adventure of
living every day, we
owe much to our dogs.

They hold back just a bit, as if to suggest they may have had enough of our foolishness. (Or are we imagining this?) They may even let out an audible sigh now and then, as if expressing resignation at our wasteful habits and confused priorities. "You're trying that again?" they seem to be silently asking us, as we attempt to repair the car ourselves, or carry an overflowing laundry basket, or roast a chicken without setting off the fire alarms. We know they are right, and appreciate the wordless commentary; it keeps us in check, even if we can't acknowledge it back to them. What a wonderful, peaceful understanding exists between us!

ABOVE Dogs think everything about us is genius.

"If you get to thinking you're a person of some influence, try ordering somebody else's dog around." —WILL ROGERS

Our dogs can be an anchor for our childhoods, but then we need to go off without them. We leave for school, college, work, and eventually our dogs pass from this world. Many of us learn about mortality and mourning from our childhood dogs as well. Separation and loss are never easy, but they make us recognize the good things in our lives, and the great gifts we have in our family and friends, in the adventure of living every day, and in the unexpected companionship we find along the way. What great teachers dogs are, in our childhood and beyond.

We start our relationships with dogs as their teachers, and before long, they become ours.

More Puppies, Please

WE'RE TALKING ABOUT THE PATTER OF LITTLE FEET, ALL FOUR OF them. Aside from the arrival of an actual human child, there are few things that cause as much giddy excitement as a new puppy in the house. It isn't even limited to the household; puppy mania has been known to overtake entire communities. "Did you hear?" the neighbors ask each other before answering their own question. "The Johnsons got a puppy." Cars slow down hoping to catch a glimpse of the new pup. Neighbors drop by uninvited, offering to help. What is it about these ridiculous creatures—they make even adult dogs seem dull by comparison.

We are programmed to go gaga over the young, to become so deliriously overcome that we are willing to put up with all the anxiety and messiness that comes

LEFT This parent dog seems relieved to have a human nanny on staff.

with them. This makes sense as it applies to human babies, but clearly it extends to all young creatures. Let's face it, even a baby snake is pretty cute. But of all creatures, puppies seem to corner the market on being unmistakably cute. Yes, we all know there are ugly babies (it's okay, they grow out of it!), but has anyone ever seen an ugly puppy? We think not.

Many of the qualities that make puppies irresistible aren't really qualities at all. They're pudgy, and clumsy, and not very smart. They eat too much. They don't know where to go the bathroom. They cry when they get lost. If these things were widely

ABOVE The joy of owning a puppy lies in watching as they discover the possibilities in the world, and in themselves.

"Training a puppy is like raising a child. Every single interaction is a training opportunity." —IAN DUNBAR

"Puppies are
constantly
inventing
new ways
to be bad…
You come
into a room
they've been
in and see
pieces of
debris and
try to figure
out what you
had that was
made from
wicker or
what had
been stuffed
with fluff."

—JULIE KLAM

regarded as positives, we'd all be much more popular than we are. But something about these little rubbery creatures makes all of these awful traits so CUTE!!! As with their human counterparts, they are capable of making us forget all of the reasonable reasons to avoid them. More puppies, please, our brains cry out.

Even puppies have lessons for us. They teach us, even as they need us to teach them. They teach us compassion and patience. They teach us the discipline that we need to teach them—the consistency, the schedule, the responsibility. Dogs learn through repetition, and so do we. It is fine that every decade or so we can be heard muttering, "What was I thinking getting a puppy??" It is good to be reminded of how helpless we are in the presence of a puppy, and how capable we are of offering

Dogs learn through repetition, and so do we.

help. When Jill Abramson, the executive editor of the *New York Times,* decided to get a puppy after her children were gone, the adventure inspired a weekly column that grew into a book. Still, what were among the first lines she wrote? "What has possessed us to do this again?" she asked herself, and her readers. Over the course of their first year together, Abramson documented the lessons learned—hers, her husband's, and the puppy's. "How much a dog learns and changes in the first year

Puppies look to us
for guidance, and
we work to live up to
their expectations.

ABOVE Like baby photos, puppy pics fill people with joy—or feigned dread.

is breathtaking," she concluded. "The puppy months can almost kill you. And then, in the blink of an eye, they are fully grown and completely attached to you. It is impossible to quantify the amount of love and work that goes into this human-dog transaction."

But not all of our friends are as enthralled as we are as we recount the joys of our new puppy: So soft! So fluffy! So smart! So energetic! So troublesome! The writer Caroline Knapp described the scene: "You'll reach into your wallet to brandish a photograph of a new puppy, and a friend will say, 'Oh, no—not pictures.'" These days it isn't just a photo in our wallet: they are on our phones and taking over our entire social media feed. We quickly learn who we can "talk puppy" with, and who just doesn't want to hear any more. We begin to understand that the question "How are you?" might just be a polite greeting and not intended to mean "How is your puppy?"

LEFT Watching a puppy discover the world, we rediscover the world ourselves.

ABOVE Dogs never quite lose their inner pup.

Some people think puppies lose their charms as they grow older, but nothing could be further from the truth. They get smarter, and they get to know you and the world's expectations better, but they never completely lose that inner pup. We may see it less often, but it still emerges: on the first snowfall of winter, at the unexpected sight of a misplaced toy, when old friends come for a visit. Imagine the joy we could express at these events if only we allowed ourselves the wild emotional abandon of puppyhood.

Dogs age faster than us, and there is always an awkward moment when their maturity in dog years surpasses our own. We are still in charge, but they are older,

"Buy a pup and
your money
will buy love
unflinching."

—RUDYARD KIPLING

With a puppy around,
even the coldest day
seems warm.

and in their own way wiser, than us. But we still call them our puppy. If they were human, this would surely cause embarrassed protestations, the way human children insist, at a certain point, they are now adults.

As dogs enter their senior years, they can regain other aspects of their youth. Things become simpler. They aren't as agile. Once easy tasks may require our assistance again, like figuring out the stairs. While we once felt a little bit of heartbeat at

No matter their age, they'll always remain "our puppy."

"There is no
psychiatrist
in the world
like a puppy
licking your
face."

—BEN WILLIAMS

their developing independence, now we feel it as their dependence on us increases again. But what a joy to be needed again—and to be able be there for our dogs, loyal to each other to the end.

They can be challenging, but their loyalty and companionship never waver. As with any important relationship in our lives, we define ourselves through what we mean to them. We are their guides and their protectors. They are our touchstones, a reminder of our own connection to the natural world. This is why, no matter what their age, they remain "our puppy" until the end.

Puppies love to explore,
but they look to us for
guidance.

Lucky Dogs

IF YOU WERE LUCKY, SOMEWHERE IN YOUR YOUTH THERE WAS A DOG who let you follow him as he trespassed through the neighborhood. You know the one: everyone knew him, because sooner or later he showed up in your mother's garden, at the public swimming pool, or wandering the aisles of the local grocery store. He showed up at children's birthday parties and backyard barbecues, and even though everyone knew he didn't belong there, no one rushed him out because of a mixture of his misplaced confidence and the sheer joy he had in being somewhere he didn't belong. He may have known the rules and the boundaries of his life, but he wasn't going to let them get in the way of his sense of adventure.

LEFT Everyone knows a dog who happily wandered the neighborhood.

There were things this dog could show you: the stinkiest garbage pail on the block; the most fragrant garden to roll in; the shade of a tree on the hill with the best vantage point in town; a trail just beyond the tree line that you hadn't realized was always there. Dogs like these love to show off their discoveries, pausing now and then to check that you are still with them, and that you see, and understand, what they are sharing with you. They are the doggiest of dogs—they miss nothing, experience everything, and sleep soundly at the end of the day.

In some cultures, wandering dogs are regarded almost as fellow citizens, roaming as they please, joining diners at restaurants and cafes, running in the surf at

ABOVE Dogs can show us the things we might otherwise overlook, even in our own backyards.

If you were lucky, somewhere in your youth was a dog who encouraged you to be a bit wilder.

"Dogs are often happier than men simply because the simplest things are the greatest things for them!"

—MEHMET MURAT ILDAN

"A dog is grateful for what is, which I am finding to be the soundest kind of wisdom and very good theology."

—CARRIE NEWCOMER

ABOVE This trail,
they seem to be sug-
gesting, will be much
more interesting.

the local beach. Friends send pictures of them gathered around a cocktail party or napping next to their chaise.

"We spent the week with these dogs," they might tell you, talking as if these were old friends introducing them to the sights and sounds of their new hometown.

Of course, part of the romance of the dog who seems to live on his own terms depends on our knowledge that, in the end, no harm will come to him. We want to see his scrappiness, his sense of wonder and adventure, but we don't want him to wander too far from the watchful eye of his family and the safety of the neighborhood who regards him as their own. We want to see in him the sense of adventure we had in our childhoods, when stepping just outside of our own yards filled us with a sense of wonder and awe.

"The greatest pleasure of a dog is that you may make a fool of yourself with him and not only will he not scold you, but he will make a fool of himself too."

—SAMUEL BUTLER

If you were lucky, you stayed in an old hotel, where the strange innkeeper nodded off early and slept in late, and while she was sleeping, her dog, whose name you never really knew, would find you alone in your room. Maybe your parents were off for the evening, or maybe they left you by yourself in order to spend some time alone in the next room. Somehow the nameless innkeeper's dog sensed this in common, and with your door left intentionally ajar, there was no way to keep him from joining you as you watched TV, or played cards, or read aloud from books that had been left behind by other travelers. And this dog's face became so human to you, you had to give him a human name, like McGillicuddy.

Fearless curiosity—just one
of the many qualities in dogs
that inspire us.

There's a romance about a dog
who lives on his own terms.

Dogs like these live on in their own timeless mythology, even after they are gone. James Thurber wrote frequently about his childhood dog, who was known to bring home all kinds of random, possibly stolen, objects, including an entire dresser that he dragged up the stairs one night. More recently, Lena Dunham wrote of how her parents' childhood dogs figured in her own young imagination. "One of the first sentences I learned was 'Cindy was a bad dog,'" she wrote. Based on her parents' memories, she concluded that dogs were "outcasts, kooks . . . not man's best friend but, rather, the mischievous sidekicks of misunderstood children."

We all love stories of dogs who get themselves into and out of trouble, even if
we prefer that they aren't our own. We love their curiosity, their bravery, their joie de
vivre, as the French poodles say. We love to share those stories, about a neighbor's
dog who ate the roast, or figured out how to turn on the bathtub faucet, or somehow
tunneled from the garage into the living room while the humans were out just a little
too late with friends. Yet the truth is, we're equally happy to tell embarrassing stories
of our own: the labrador that refuses to swim, the vicious chihuahua, the well-trained
dog that refuses to demonstrate any tricks when he knows there is an audience.

We don't want even our scrappiest dogs to wander too far from the safety of the neighborhood.

"Dogs and philosophers do the greatest good and get the fewest rewards."

—DIOGENES

Lucky dogs know no boundaries
to their sense of adventure.

What is it about these dogs that inspires our forgiveness? And beyond that, what is it about their seeming defiance that sometimes makes us respect them just a little bit more? What makes these troublemakers seem so lucky to us, when logic suggests that they are really getting by on the whim of fate? It must be their childlike sense of wonder that takes us back to when something as simple as a mud puddle could be fascinating and we didn't care about getting wet. These dogs are so genuinely engaged in the world around them, we cannot help but stand back and take note. They live without regrets, and without false modesty, and in doing so, they let us all become children again.

ABOVE Our canine companions help us maintain a childlike sense of wonder.

"... sometimes I'll be the littlest kid with my dog and marvel at his ears and his nose and how he looks at me."

—AARON ECKHART

They say cats have nine lives, but it is really dogs who get lucky. By the end of their lives they have such long, inspiring lists of adventures. Even when they slow down later in life, they can surprise us, in the best, messiest of ways: rolling in a stinky pile of fish along a river, raiding a dumpster down the street, deconstructing that too expensive jacket that (they are right) we really shouldn't have bought. They do it with such gusto, it would be impossible not to award them with our deepest respect.

Dogs' curiosity can lead them to some extraordinarily surprising friendships.

Roadtripping

EVER SINCE 1903, WHEN HORATIO NELSON JACKSON MADE THE FIRST cross-country drive in an automobile—and picked up a stray pit bull to ride shotgun—dogs and road trips have been cemented in our nation's collective consciousness as one of the most quintessentially American phenomena. There were no highways back then—and not many roads for automobiles—so Horatio and Bud had their work cut out for them, cutting across fields, getting stuck in the mud, but keeping each other safe the whole way along.

Dogs have long been our companions as we explore the frontier, and the automobile brought the idea into a new age. No wonder then that we continue to travel with our favorite dogs at our side. It is no longer out of necessity that we explore

LEFT Nothing beats the feel of the wind against your jowls.

beyond our community's boundaries, and the dangers are not the same as they once were, but we still want to share our experiences with our canine companions. Our mobility is a privilege, and as with so many other privileges, it is one that our dogs have earned the right to share.

Were hatchbacks invented for loading groceries . . . or dogs? Many of us may remember our childhood dogs riding in the back-back of the family station wagon, but these days we are just as likely to see them riding alongside the human passengers. There are dog seat belts, and dog car harnesses, and ramps to help older dogs up to the seat. There are even cars designed specifically for dog owners, because to be the owner of a car and a dog is to always be engaged in the intersection of the two.

Where are all these dogs going? To pick up kids from school. To run a few errands at local stores. To visit with their friends at the park. Depending on where

ABOVE Traveling can be an endurance test, but with the right companions, everyone enjoys the ride.

"To a dog, motoring isn't just a way of getting from here to there, it's also a thrill and an adventure. The mere jingle of car keys is enough to send most any dog into a whimpering, tail-wagging frenzy."

—JON WINOKUR

Many of us remember
our dogs riding in the
back with us.

you live, they may be accompanying their people to a dog-friendly bar, or society ball. Some, like a colicky baby, may just need (or demand) a drive around the block to calm down.

An individual dog's relationship to cars may be one of the things that separates him from the pack. Some will jump into any stranger's car or taxi given the chance. Others blanch at the notion of giving up that much control—who knows where this vehicle might take them? It could end up being a visit with the vet instead of a romp on the beach! And some share both these traits: willing to jump inside, but grabbing the wheel to drive once the car gets moving. Truckers, who drive long hours across the country, often have a devoted dog in their cab and are some of the best

ABOVE Hurry up, humans. We're about to throw this thing into gear.

ABOVE Some dogs are more adventurous than others, but if it has wheels, it's worth a try.

dog owners around; when you spend that much time together, you're bound to be inspired to do some spoiling.

Traveling with our dogs is such an essential aspect of living, we begin to practice early by carting our dogs around the yard in our childhood wagons, exploring our own tiny frontier. Even if we don't have pets of our own, we practice the task using plush toy animals, which surely are the best behaved pet travelers anyone has ever had. As adults, our travels become more diverse, but in many cases our pets continue to journey alongside us. Airlines feature pet travel services with special, dedicated staff; trains have become pet-friendly; but it is the hotel and resort industry that has gone all out to welcome canine travelers with a full menu of services. Need a

The universal expression
of a satisfied traveler.

"I've always thought a hotel ought to offer optional small animals. I mean a cat to sleep on your bed at night, or a dog of some kind to act pleased when you come in. You ever notice how a hotel room feels so lifeless?" —ANNE TYLER, *THE ACCIDENTAL TOURIST*

doggie tuck in while you are out? No problem. Canine room service? They have that covered, too! Dog walking and doggie daycare? Certainly.

The options are nearly as grandiose for dogs we choose to leave behind: forget the human resorts, now dogs have their own dog boarding facilities with program directors to rival any cruise. They can choose between a Junior or Executive Suite, enroll in playgroups, and spend their time lounging undisturbed in the sun (with sunscreen liberally applied by the staff). Some facilities have individual televisions

ABOVE Whether by land or by sea, some dogs sure do get around.

ABOVE Certain kinds of traveling, such as a move, can make dogs anxious.

and couches and bunks. It's possible, when you check into a hotel room alone, to recognize that your dogs are staying in a larger space—and possibly at a higher rate—than your own.

As much as we enjoy traveling together, there are few things as gut-wrenching as an actual move. A packed suitcase can induce a dog's nerves, but an unpacked closet causes a near breakdown. Dogs love routine, and we may secretly love them for enforcing a routine on our otherwise chaotic lives. Taking that routine—the three

"Charley is a mind-reading dog. There have been many trips in his lifetime, and often he has to be left at home. He knows we are going long before the suitcase has come out, and he paces and worries and whines and goes into a state of mild hysteria."

—JOHN STEINBECK,
TRAVELS WITH CHARLEY

Traveling with our dogs is
an essential part of living.

walks a day, the meals and bedtime—on our travels keeps a sense of home with us. But an actual move throws everything off, for us and for them. We have an advantage of knowing that all of these pieces that are being disassembled and packed up will be put back together again.

That's what makes home so valuable to us. We love the routine and the rituals. We want the fuss of our dogs when we open the door. Maybe that's part of what makes our travels, with or without our dogs, so rewarding: we are reminded of everything we care about at home.

ABOVE An individual dog's relationship to cars may be one of the things that separates him from the pack.

When we travel, we are reminded of everything we care about at home.

When Horatio Nelson Jackson and his dog Bud made their way across the US more than a hundred years ago, they became instant celebrities, their portraits splashed across the front page of newspapers in every town they drove through. They had spent $8,000 in order to win a $50 bet, but they also managed to reinvent the American tradition of expanding a frontier, and Bud's contribution was just as important as any mechanic or map.

Bud was, Jackson said, "The one member of our trio who used no profanity on the entire trip."

Dogs and roadtrips
are a quintessentially
American combination.

Good Sports

IF THERE'S ANYTHING DOGS SEEM UNIVERSALLY PROGRAMMED TO perform, it is the act of fetching. Whether it is a ball or a stick or the newspaper, the act of bringing these objects "home" to drop at our feet is such a stereotype that we really only find it remarkable when a dog fails to perform. Pity the poor dog who has no game, the one who watches as the ball is thrown and then just continues waiting, completely uninspired to retrieve it, or, perhaps, waiting for you to go get the toy and bring it back to him.

It is said that dogs learn through repetition. The truth is we humans learn through repetition as well. It isn't just learning, it is soothing. Routines like these are calming, a sort of meditation that incorporates our bodies as well as our minds. Did man teach the dog to fetch, or was it the other way around?

LEFT Dogs remind us that the world is full of simple pleasures.

Of course, so many of the behaviors of play between humans and dogs are tied to our history of using dogs as companions for hunting. In "Men and Their Dogs," Paul Fersen writes, "There is a myth out there that the loss of a great hunting dog is psychologically as devastating to a man as the loss of a spouse. Unquestionably this originated in a posturing haze of scotch and testosterone around a campfire somewhere, but it speaks volumes about the relationship of a hunter and his dog . . . . Talk to hunters about their dogs and you will hear praise of such an effusive nature, one would think they were offspring, but even children seldom receive the plaudits reserved for a great dog in hunting circles."

Our dogs bear witness to the natural world around us.

ABOVE Hunting gives us another excuse to spend time with our dogs.

"For us hunting wasn't a sport. It was a way to be intimate with nature."

—TED KERASOTE, *MERLE'S DOOR*

"The literature of dogs has mostly become a literature of longing: for home, for safety, for acceptance, and probably for some flicker of the wildness we ourselves have lost." —BRONWEN DICKEY

Dogs on a hunt provide assistance by using their superior sense to track their prey, or to retrieve, but their primary usefulness in the field may be simply to be our companions. Much of the time we spend hunting is spent, more or less, not hunting. Hunting means hiking and quiet contemplation; it is a retreat from the contemporary world. The dogs' role is not only to lead us to the game, but also to keep us safe, to bear witness to nature alongside us, and ultimately, to accompany us back home.

Writing in *Troubles with Bird Dogs,* George Bird Evans said, "I think we are drawn to dogs because they are the uninhibited creatures we might be if we weren't certain we knew better. They fight for honor at the first challenge, make love with

no moral restraint, and they do not for all their marvelous instincts appear to know about death."

Their sense of sport is distilled. Their every display is balanced perfectly between being purposeful and being just "why not." They have the ego to show off their perfect mid-air catch and the patience to recognize that a day spent fishing isn't necessarily a day wasted even if no fish are caught. Even when the sport is dog-on-dog play, the joy in watching them is to see them take turns being on top; dogs, with their non-competitive spirit, would make the perfect Olympians. Just watch dogs in competition in agility and you know this is true; there may be ribbons and trophies to be won, but their focus is on the immediate goal of achieving their own personal best.

Executing the perfect
midair catch.

"The dog was created specially for children. He is the god of frolic."

—HENRY WARD BEECHER

The origin of fetch.

Dogs that have been taught a skill know that there is a time and place to perform it, and observers can sense the excitement rising in the dogs when they arrive at the designated arena. You can see their focus intensify and their muscles twitch, waiting for the signal to begin. It is then that they become fully alive: jetting over and under, or running into the "outfield" to catch a frisbee and return. They aren't performing for the audience, though they may acknowledge that they are there. This moment is purely about them.

Dogs excel not only at athletic challenges, but at mind games as well—not the mind games that people play with each other socially, but challenges that tax their

BELOW A dog's sense of smell helps him find things we might overlook.

ABOVE Dogs never act like they have seen it all or chased their toys too many times.

mental capacities: food puzzles and scent work, where they are trained to track a variety of scents and signal when they have found them. Sometimes, dogs seem to teach themselves how to track scents on their own, and the scents that appeal to them are sometimes alarming: a rotting fish discarded in the tall reeds along a river bed; the poop dropped by another species in their yard. We can't ask them what it is that appeals to them, but some theorize their instinct is to disguise themselves by covering up their own smell.

Dogs are great guides for us, whether we are on a traditional hunt or just seeking to find that elusive, misplaced, primal bond with the natural world around us.

"The most affectionate creature in the world is a wet dog."

—AMBROSE BIERCE

"The friendship of a dog is precious. It becomes even more so when one is so far removed from home…. I have a Scottie. In him I find consolation and diversion… he is the one person to whom I can talk without the conversation coming back to war."

—DWIGHT D. EISENHOWER

They never stop finding joy in what we mistake as ordinary. They never feel that they have seen it all. Dogs are rarely jaded.

This is fantastic, they seem to say, as they run for the ball one more time, or track the scent of another animal, or watch as we cast our nets and rods again after coming up empty one more time. They remind us of what we shouldn't need to be reminded of at all: that this world is full of simple pleasures, and all we need to do to be a part of it is step outside and let our senses lead the way.

Like their human counterparts, dogs slow down as they grow older, and as their endurance levels shift, so do their interests. But they never actually lose their

ABOVE By keeping our dogs active, we reinforce our bond with them.

> "A door is
> what a dog
> is perpetually
> on the wrong
> side of."
>
> —OGDEN NASH

interest in interacting with the world and exerting their influence upon it. As their guardians, we need to recognize this and facilitate new forms of play. Some easy ways to do this: incorporate affordable treadmills instead of jogging, food puzzles in place of hiking, and stairs or ramps for getting into the car or bed where they once could just leap. By keeping our dogs both physically and mentally active—whatever their abilities—we can continue to reinforce that bond between us and show that regardless of circumstance we really are "dog's best friend."

Dogs never stop finding
joy in what we mistake
as ordinary.

Running with the Pack

THE POSITIVE HEALTH BENEFITS OF COMPANION ANIMALS HAVE LONG
been established: they lower our blood pressure, decrease stress, improve mental
health, and increase longevity—and that's before they even get us out of bed in
the morning. We've said that our animals reconnect us to the natural world, and this
often occurs in the most literal way: walking around the neighborhood together, or
exploring the mountains and valleys and geography around us. And for many people, it is the dog who gently takes the lead. Increasingly, the first step for a success-
ful personal fitness program is the introduction of a canine partner.

Nick Trout, a veterinarian who also writes (and runs), stated it best: "Enter the
best personal trainer you might ever find—your dog! Think about it: no need to

LEFT The first step in
starting a fitness program
is soliciting the help of a
canine partner.

make polite conversation and no one to ask, 'Do these shorts make my butt look fat?' And best of all, your dog is probably a cheery incentive consistently loitering at your front door." But our dogs' silence also gives us an extra responsibility on our outdoor excursions: we need to be aware of their needs—for rest, for water—because they can't tell us on their own. But this requirement—that we think outside of our own needs and experiences—is a gift rather than a burden. Whatever our relationship with our dogs, it is their dependence on us that also allows us to heal.

The simple demands of companionship can nudge us toward more positive habits for ourselves. Dogs are such creatures of habit, it makes them ideal assistants

ABOVE The positive health benefits of dogs are well known.

"Petting, scratching and cuddling a dog could be as soothing to the mind and heart as deep meditation and almost as good for the soul as prayer." —DEAN KOONTZ

"My dog friends seem to understand my limitations, and always keep close beside me when I'm alone. I love their affectionate ways and the eloquent wag of their tails." —HELEN KELLER

ABOVE We need to be aware of our dog's need for rest and water on long excursions.

for us. Their talent at observation, and their pleasure in maintaining the status quo, make them brilliant at being trained to serve us in specialized roles.

Everyone knows about dogs that serve the blind, guiding them safely on the street and signaling at hazards that their master cannot understand on their own. But for a service dog to work successfully, both parties have to be trained. "Interdependence has long seemed to me the ideal in a relationship," writer Amy Hempel once shared. "Dogs have always taken good care of me and vice versa." Her respect for this mutually rewarding bond inspired her to begin volunteering to train dogs for Guiding Eyes for the Blind. "What we puppy raisers can do for the blind people who will come to rely on these dogs is build the dogs' confidence and base

"The world would be a nicer place if everyone had the ability to love as un-conditionally as a dog."

—M.K. CLINTON

of experience: We introduce them to a wide range of situations and activities, we get them used to being groomed and handled, we teach them good manners, we see that they have fun and enjoy their work. Every moment is intensified because of the impending separation, which can make a walk in the park almost unendurably poignant. Luckily, these pups are hilarious and unfailingly game, and reside entirely in the moment."

Dogs' ability to watch out for us extends beyond assisting the sight-impaired; dogs can also be trained to assist people who suffer from epilepsy. Actress Mary Tyler Moore has a dog who is so keenly observant he can warn her when her blood sugar is too low. Other dogs have been able to detect cancer. How is that possible?

The companionship of
dogs always leads us to
our better selves.

Even in the most gorgeous
surroundings, dogs turn
their attention back to us.

Perhaps it's due to the fact that dog noses have 300 million sensors, compared to our own measly 5 million.

Dogs are also trained more formally to perform public safety roles: police dogs and search and rescue dogs are able to detect potential dangers or rescue people from harm. This role goes back at least as far as 1888, when bloodhounds were used to assist in the hunt for serial killer Jack the Ripper. Because of their hunting skills, dogs were eventually trained for specific purposes in the Armed Forces as well as to be sentries, messengers, and scouts.

One of the most extraordinary developments of the role canines play in healing has been their use in supporting veterans suffering from post-traumatic stress after serving our country. David Sharpe is an Air Force veteran who started Compan-

ABOVE Dogs make great partners in reflection.

ABOVE Dogs can bear witness to our quietest moments.

ions for Heroes after his own experience with PTSD and the healing power of a pit bull puppy companion whose presence at his side helped diminish the emotional outbursts he previously struggled to control. Testifying before Congress, Sharpe explained the simple power of this relationship: "It was Cheyenne who was the force that pulled me back into society. I couldn't talk to anybody—not my father, not the counselors—but I can talk to my shelter dog, and she never judges me."

Terms like PTSD and "emotional support dog" may be new, but the healing power of our canine companions hasn't really changed. Maybe our understanding and appreciation has increased as we, the humans, get a bit smarter. But our dogs have

"Interdependence has long seemed to me the ideal in a relationship. Dogs have always taken good care of me and vice versa."

—AMY HEMPEL

How do dogs always
manage to be in the
present moment?

been serving us in these same ways for centuries, and their sense of duty has been pure, whether or not we gave them a formal title for their jobs. A dog doesn't seem to need any special training to stay close when we aren't feeling well, or if our mood is down. That's when they find a careful position from which to observe us, and wait, like the most dedicated companions do, until we are well enough to return to our old, reassuring routines, and leave the house again.

The companionship of dogs always leads us to our better selves. How do they manage it, other than their ability to always be present in the moment, undistract-

ABOVE A dog's love is pure, regardless of size or breed.

> "The reason a dog has so many friends is that he wags his tail instead of his tongue."
>
> —UNKNOWN

ed by politics or ambition? Dogs don't change careers. They aren't working their way up the social ladder (at least not outside of our yard). They aren't interested in our connections, or our resumes, or where we went to school. They aren't impressed by fancy houses, or fashion, or any passing fads. Dogs see only the purest form of their companions, and they marvel at it. Imagine if we all managed to do the same, too.

Dogs see only the
purest form of their
companions.

A Dog's Napping Is Never Done

IF YOU WERE A DOG, RIGHT NOW YOU'D BE NAPPING. OR MEDITATING.
Or possibly meditating on the possibilities of napping—so many choices, so many positions, so many ways to turn and turn before finally settling into your chosen nest. It is often said that dogs do everything with gusto, and that determined enthusiasm isn't limited to activities. Dogs can nap like no one else.

Our dogs are great examples for us to follow in so many ways, but perhaps their greatest gift is the example they set in how to spend leisure time. Yes, they are athletes. Yes, they may be working dogs who dedicate themselves to a task, yet in any case our dogs are always aware that life is about balance. Work, then rest. Play, then rest. Daydream, then rest. They allow themselves authority over how they

LEFT Dog beds are nice, but so are any number of other spots for a snooze.

spend their day, and they seem intent on making sure that nothing goes unappreciated. They are dedicated to being their best, and they understand, more than we do, that being your best requires an appreciation of all aspects of a day and all aspects of our lives: the restless and the calm, the noisy and the quiet.

If you were a dog, right now you'd be stretching in the sun. Dogs are such masters at yoga, they even have a pose named after them. Rising from a nap, dogs do the things we humans need to do but so often ignore. They stretch. They take a

ABOVE Dogs can make themselves comfortable anywhere.

"A dog teaches a boy fidelity, perseverance, and to turn around three times before lying down." —ROBERT BENCHLEY

"Whoever said let sleep-
ing dogs lie didn't sleep
with dogs." —UNKNOWN

ABOVE No bed,
cushion, laundry
bag, or hammock
is left untested.

few breaths. They collect themselves and get a drink of water before finding a task. We could learn so much by following their example. But we don't. We admire them and their routines, but then we return to our own counterintuitive habits. We try to work long past the point of fatigue. We climb out of bed and get the day going at top gear. We forget to drink water. Imagine our heightened efficiency if we took our cues from the dogs. Stretch when they stretch. Rest when they rest. Work with the diligence and authority they bring to a bone. Pour a glass of water any time we hear them lapping at a bowl.

If you were a dog, right now you'd be lying in the cool earth under the shade of your favorite tree. Sure, it might be a little damp and dirty, but there isn't a softer or more inviting bed. Try it. Close your eyes and feel the earth resting against your body and smell the freshly cut grass. Relax your body further into the surface and listen. Everything is so quiet, but it feels as if you can hear every tiny sound.

Dogs sleep about half their lives; some sleep as much as eighteen hours in a day. But we never have the sense that they are escaping things, because the time they are awake is lived full-tilt. Nothing is left unexamined. Nothing is untasted. Not a moment is wasted. Dogs' lives are short; they don't fool around with time. Even

"You never see a dog with a wristwatch." —GEORGE CARLIN

Do our dogs ever dream of us?

while they are sleeping they seem to keep going, muttering to themselves or to the phantoms of their dreams, their legs gently pedaling the air.

Who are they running from, we wonder as we watch them, rapt. Or to whom are they trying to catch up?

Do they ever dream, we may wonder, of us?

If you were a dog, right now you wouldn't be worried about what time it is—at least that's what the experts say. Dogs, they claim, have no sense of time. But if that is true, how is it that they have such a keen ability to measure out the portions of their day? They know just how much to play, how much to run, how much to rest, and how much to consider everything that they've done. If they had no sense of

ABOVE Dogs appreciate naps so much that even a bed of leaves is inviting.

time, would they seem as relieved to see us again after an absence? Is it the absence of time that makes them live so purely in the now?

If you were a dog, right now you'd be burrowed between the cushions of the couch. Or lying at your master's feet. If you were a dog, you wouldn't have any regrets to distract you from appreciating all that was in front of you. You would understand that the world really is a pretty amazing place, and that all of your senses were just enough to know what your place was here. That's a pretty awesome feeling to have as you close your eyes for another nap.

Dogs are aware that
life is about balance.
Work, then rest. Play,
then rest.

"A dog naps so much
because he loves so
hard." —UNKNOWN

If you were a dog,
you might be under
the table lying near
your master's feet.

One of the real reasons dogs sleep so much is that they sleep very lightly. This is why they leap from what appears to be a dead sleep every time they hear an absent family member's car make the turn to return home, or when a potential intruder is lurking outside beneath a street light, or when you get up to go to the bathroom and they have to make sure that you aren't about to escape from the window. And then, miraculously, they go back to sleep. "Oh, you're home," they say, before turn-

Don't worry,
I'm just resting.

> "It is naught good a sleeping hound to wake."
>
> —GEOFFREY CHAUCER

ing three times and switching off like a light. "Oh, he's not breaking in." "Oh, you're just using that water thing again." Meanwhile, we sit up half the night.

Do dogs ever have insomnia? Maybe it is their perpetual state, but they have the sense—and the ability—to stop and get some zees at any time and in any place. They may have their favorite places to snooze—in the living room, in our laps, at the foot of the bed—but if necessary, they don't hesitate to get a bit of rest anywhere they might find themselves with time: on a crowded sidewalk, under the table of a cafe, in a boat. They are an inspiration to those of us from whom sleep hides.

Dogs are an inspiration for
the insomniacs among us.

The Four Seasons of Dog

SPRING IS FLOWERS AND SUNSHINE AND LONGER DAYS. SPRING SEEMS
to be the season of puppies, though truthfully puppies own every part of the year.
But spring is also known as the season of mud. Like childbirth, or raising a puppy,
mud is one of those recurring trials in our lives that we erase from memory because
otherwise we might never move forward. So every spring we are reminded, all
over again, what it means to have dogs and mud. They track it into our houses, and
into our cars, and onto our furniture, and even into our beds. Nothing shows how
much we love our dogs as much as sliding between our winter comforter at night
to discover it's been layered with spring mud. There may be a moment of outrage,
then acceptance, and then, almost as quickly, we are working the experience into

LEFT Dogs lead us to
appreciate the seasons.

an anecdote for friends, because we know this is what we signed up for when we brought these dogs into our lives. This mud is love.

Secretly, we admire their recklessness. They don't worry about creating a mess. They don't fear discovering what lies buried beneath the winter muck. They don't hesitate to literally stop and smell the roses, inserting their wondrous snouts directly to the base of the bloom, where the bees also buzz.

Oh, to be as liberated as dogs are, even in domesticity. To see a mud puddle and instead of navigating the perimeter, just jump!

Dogs, no matter their region, are all Southerners at heart. They understand that summer—apart from two brief periods around Memorial Day and Labor Day—is

ABOVE Spring seems to be the season of puppies.

Secretly, we admire our dogs' recklessness.

Dogs understand that summer is not meant for working.

not meant for working. We'd do well to follow their example. What's the rush about everything? It's hot out, the air is thick, and only dogs and Southerners are smart enough to recognize that there's nothing sinful about slowing down. There's nothing so urgent that it can't wait until October, so we may as well all find a good shady spot for napping, a stack of good books to chew on, and a bowl of our favorite water or a cocktail.

Dogs in summer are at their most Zen. It's all about being present and still. It's the sound of insects and tree frogs, and of the children playing down the street. It's about anticipating thunder and making it through to the other side of the storm. Unlike us, dogs don't enter summer with a list of expectations that will be missed.

ABOVE Oh, to be as liberated as dogs are!

They don't have summer travel goals, or a list of chores and renovations they think will somehow be easier to do while the kids are home. That look your dog gives you when you meet with an architect about the kitchen and landscaper about the lawn—it's not a look of confusion; he's trying to tell you to slow it down.

There's still plenty to enjoy, even at a slower pace. Remember, the days are longer. There's time early in the morning for a nice walk as soon as it gets light, and extra time in the evening to hang out on the deck. And that still leaves room for a good long nap when the afternoon heat is at its peak. Don't feel guilty; this is how we're supposed to live.

Dogs in summer are
at their most Zen.

"A good dog never dies. He always stays. He walks besides you on crisp autumn days when frost is on the fields and winter's drawing near." —MARY CAROLYN DAVIES

ABOVE All that mischief that was dormant in the summer comes back in the fall.

Those more reasonable temperatures of autumn are always welcome, but then we're in for a shock. What happened to the mellow dogs of summer? They are gone, and the spirit and energy of puppy dogs have taken their place, no matter what their chronological age. All that mischief that was dormant for summer is now back, and we just have to get used to it. As temperatures dip, our dogs' enthusiasm for life goes up. There are leaves and spoiled garden vegetables to roll in. There are fall yard parties to crash. And there are weekends, which seemed to blur into weeks over the summer, but now pop with the distinct energy of having everyone finally home.

ABOVE Wherever dogs go, there are people to find.

Why does fall seem like the perfect season? Wherever dogs go, there are people to find. At home, in the yard, at the park—the world is alive. And there is football, which means tailgating, which means food being dropped on the ground, food that no one will ever miss if you are fast enough. Dogs generally like their good deeds to be rewarded, but this particular cleaning duty is a reward in itself.

Dogs, unlike humans, seem to consider whatever season they are in to be the best of all. But there may be another reason dogs love autumn: October is an adopt-a-shelter-dog month. Who can argue with that?

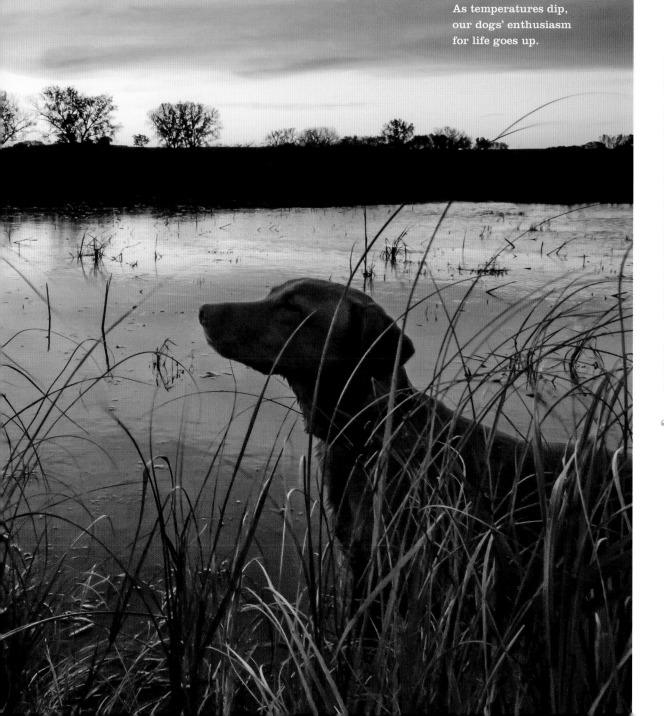

As temperatures dip, our dogs' enthusiasm for life goes up.

"A dog can't think that much about what he's doing; he just does what feels right."

—BARBARA KINGSOLVER

Our dogs are here to
remind us that winter
isn't so bad.

For some people, the best thing about winter is that it means spring is eventually coming back around again. Our dogs are here to remind us that things aren't so bad. In fact, this is a duty they fulfill year round. Are the days shorter? Yes. Is it cold out? Yes. Are snow and ice getting in the way of all of our supposedly important commitments? Yes. But our dogs are here with us, ready to bound outdoors and remind us that perhaps these things aren't as important as they seem. Cold

Cold weather can easily be overcome by activity—and eating some snow.

Winters never
seem their coldest
when there is a dog
at our side.

weather can easily be overcome by activity, and snow can be overcome by sticking our faces in and eating it.

Dogs are built differently than we are. This is no surprise. But they really can lead us to appreciate the seasons and the elements with a degree of patience we might not otherwise have. On our own, we aim to find some leverage over the environment that contains us. With dogs as our partners, we can open up to the opportunities the elements offer, for play, for the practicalities of living, and for living in the moment and appreciating the beauty of being alive.

Winters never seem their coldest when there is a dog at our side.

Dogs seem to consider
whatever season they
are in the best of all.

"Dogs think
everyday is
Christmas."

—RAY BRADBURY

Coming Home

FOR THOSE OF US WHO WERE RAISED AMONG DOG PEOPLE, THE definition of what constitutes a family will always include at least one dog. For us, dogs are a constant, that one thing upon which everyone can agree, in spite of all of our other differences. Who is waiting for us when we get back from an errand or from work or from school? Our dogs. And while they may have missed us while we were gone, when we are present they remind us that this is all that matters: this time together, this space that we share. Dogs live in the present, and those of us who are lucky enough to share our lives with dogs get that daily reminder that all those "other" things are rarely as important as what is directly in front of us now: our family, our friends, our home, our bone.

LEFT For many of us, the definition of family will always include one dog.

Our dogs are one of the comforts that make leaving home more difficult—at least when we have to leave without them. While many dogs take our routine farewells in stride, others seem a bit alarmed that we might be forgetting to take them with us. Again. What could possibly warrant our departure, they may wonder? And what might become of us, they seem to be thinking, without their help navigating the world?

Dogs, with all of their curiosity and their powerful senses, also know the allure of returning to what is most familiar and comforting. To them, routine isn't boring: it is nature's greatest reward. Certainly they have nothing against adventure, but the

ABOVE Who is waiting for us when we come home from school or work? Our dogs.

"Once you have had a wonderful dog, a life without one, is a life diminished."

—DEAN KOONTZ

"Without dogs, our houses are cold receptacles for things. Dogs make a fire warmer with their curled presence. They wake us, greet us, protect us, and ultimately carve a place in our hearts and our history." —PAUL FERSEN

ABOVE In a true dog
lover's home, dogs are
always allowed on the
couch.

end of any adventure, as we learn in all legends and children's books, is when we get to return home. They never get bored of us or their friends; they see no need to redecorate or move; they are perfectly happy eating the same thing every day and napping in the same spot and finding such enormous excitement exploring the same yard morning, noon, and night. This is one of their lessons for us: whatever you do, don't forget about home.

Certainly this magnetic pull our dogs hold on us must be why we choose to take them along with us, or arrange for someone else to spoil them while we are gone. We may drop them off at doggy daycare, or leave them with a sitter armed with a

> "A dog is so
> often the
> answer—
> when you're
> lonely and
> need compa-
> ny, or when
> you're tired
> of company
> and need
> lonely."
>
> —ROBERT BRAULT

supply of favorite treats and a two-page list of their favorite things, but increasingly, we bring our dogs along, because it is a way of bringing home along with us too. The comforts our dogs supply at home, it turns out, can join us on the road. And in the office. At our favorite cafe. On the beach. At the park. On a hike.

And the best surprise of all: our dogs can break down barriers between us and the strangers we meet along the way—strangers who turn out to be just like us and speak the same language we do: the language of people who love their dogs. Home isn't limited to the place where we sleep; it includes the parks and cafes and open spaces that we visit with our dogs throughout the week. Anyone who

Our dogs are always ready to lead us on
an adventure and take us back home.

Dogs find excitement exploring the same backyard morning, noon, and night.

frequents a dog park knows how much like family that community can feel. In his memoir, *Off the Leash*, Matthew Gilbert writes, "Dogs bring us into our own hearts but they are also a bridge to other people. It's a cliché, I totally know that . . . . And yet there it is: my truth and the truth of many dog owners I've gotten to know." We share our joys and our heartbreak with people whose one connection to us is our shared love of dogs.

Living in a world that includes our animal companions makes it hard to ever feel lost or alone. They are more than accessories. They comfort us when the world gets to be too much. They slow us down when the world gets too busy. They get us on our feet when we become lazy. They love us when we feel unworthy.

BELOW Living with dogs makes it hard to ever feel alone.

Dogs are our great master regulators, capable of bringing our lives into balance—and the most masterful part of this skill is that they do it so effortlessly, it doesn't seem like work at all.

Wherever we are, if our dogs are with us, it feels like home.

Even for mortal humans, our home, whatever it may be and however we may feel about it, has an inescapable pull, and like dogs, our senses connect us to both the physical world and its inhabitants. Even things we outgrow, or perhaps actively

"The greatest
fear dogs
know is the
fear that
you will not
come back
when you
go out the
door without
them."

—STANLEY COREN

"Dogs are our bridge—our connection to who we really are, and most tellingly, who we want to be. When we call them home to us, it's as if we are calling for home itself. And that'll do, dogs. That'll do." —PATRICIA B. MCCONNELL

dislike, can trigger a sense of reassuring safety after a long absence: the distinct smell of manure from the fields at the end of town, the echoing honks of traffic in the city, the too-firm mattress of a familiar bed. All of these things and more can make us realize we are home. For dogs, these reassuring senses tie them to us and to our lives, every day. And in return, we realize in their absence the value of their gentle snore, the sound of their nails on the floor, the precise degree of pressure exerted when they heave up against us, the corn-chip scent of their paws. We can't underestimate their worth, and the space left empty when they are gone.

RIGHT Wherever we are, if our dogs are with us, it feels like home.

"Dogs bring us into our own hearts but they are also a bridge to other people."

—MATTHEW GILBERT

We should follow every dog's example and live, with them, in the moment. With dogs at our side, home is an adventure and each day brings us back to our roots: to family, friends, and trusted animals, to the familiar shade of century-old trees, to comfortable spaces and old furniture smells, and to the foods we have eaten since we were children. To the sense of wonder that binds all of us to the natural world.

Our dogs remind us of what is really important in the world, what is good and true. They bring us back to the magic that is simplicity, and we will do anything for them in return. 🦴

Those of us who share our lives with dogs are reminded that other things are rarely as important as our family, our friends, our home, our bone.

Petfinder
FOUNDATION

You donate. We match. Tails start wagging.

In 2016, Orvis looks forward to continuing our relationship with the Petfinder Foundation for the fifth consecutive year. You can help. When you donate to this cause, we match your donation. It's that simple.

The Orvis Company is partnering with its customers to help the Petfinder Foundation in its mission to support rescue shelters. Orvis will match every donation dollar for dollar up to $30,000 for a total contribution of $60,000.

To help, send your check to:

Petfinder, c/o The Orvis Company
178 Conservation Way
Sunderland, VT 05250, or donate online.

Please join us in support of the Petfinder Foundation's mission.
—Dave Perkins, Vice Chairman, The Orvis Company

THE ORVIS COMMITMENT

WE WANT TO STOP CANINE CANCER IN ITS TRACKS

Orvis Cover Dog Contest Winners